THE ROSE EFFECT:

EIGHT STEPS TO DELIVERING THE PERFORMANCE OF YOUR LIFE

THE
ROSE
EFFECT

DEDICATIONS

To my family, who has diligently and relentlessly championed my journey. Your intercessory prayers and unconditional love are the reasons I'm here today.

Thank you, Lord, for trusting me with this assignment.

Love,

Keanna

PRAISES

"When you're working with KJ, her energy just boun-ces off of her and goes straight to you. She's the best. KJ helped me to get some confidence to go out there and do a little two-step."
~ **Lil Nas X, 2x Grammy Award-winning diamond artist**

"I have watched KJ Rose begin her journey in the music industry, which started with a passion for performing and led to coaching performers worldwide. Her artistry is the culmination of 20-plus years in the music business. I have witnessed her contribution of vocals to top-selling artists as a background singer and stepping out on faith to complete an amazing solo R&B album. KJ has maintained her enthusiasm and determination to be great on all accounts. If an artist has a morsel of potential to perform, KJ Rose is certified to extract it, often helping them discover capabilities they were unaware existed. Greatness is the only option when working with The Rose Effect. I am excited to see what challenge is presented to KJ to conquer next. I'm sure she will manage it prudently."
~ **Jax, music producer, writer, and MC**

"KJ Rose has been a treasured asset at Tri Destined Studios for several years, overseeing and empowering our talent in front of and behind the camera. Her ability to make everyone feel special and worthy to be called is an anointed gift from God. She is uplifting, encouraging, intuitive, talented, and a beautifully brilliant inspiration to us all. It has been a joy to see her soar and carry others on her wings! I am elated that through the words enveloped in this book, she will now get to share more of her greatness with the world! Shine on, KJ. Shine!!!"

~Nikaya D. Brown Jones, CEO, Tri **Destined Studios**

"I don't know anyone more qualified to bring out the most positive and natural talent from an artist. Her presence is regal; therefore, her clients are able to take part in her light and reach their highest potential."

~ Phylicia Fant, Co-head of Urban Music, Columbia Records

"KJ is important to any label trying to break a new artist. She is bringing back true artist development. I've watched her be hands-on and available to the artists. This is a gift you just can't live without."

~ Shawn "Tubby" Holiday, Co-head of Urban Music, Columbia Records

"KJ Rose is the complete artist whisperer that brings out the best in her clients."

~Gee Roberson, CO-CEO The Blueprint Group

"I've had the opportunity to know Keanna from the inception of her music career. I've watched her develop as an artist , become a student of her craft, and step into her natural gift as an artist development expert. KJ's drive and commitment to bringing the absolute best performance out of her artists is unyielding and necessary."

~ Jon Platt, Chairman and CEO of Sony/ ATV Music Publishing

"I am so excited about this book and what it will do for new and experienced performers, but not just that. KJ's honesty and strength is so evident and beautiful. She shares her journey of becoming the force that she is! I love it and her. These words have the power to push you to be your greatest self, the version of you that you dream of! Thankful for this book! It's going to change lives!"

~ Erica Campbell, Grammy Award-winning gospel artist, author, actress, radio host, and First Lady of the Cali Worship Center

"KJ has the perfect combination of skill, work ethics, experience, energy, and most importantly, empathy. Those qualities enable her to turn aspiring artists into superstars and ensure that superstars continue to shine."

~ Steve Pamon, President & COO, Parkwood Entertainment

"When I worked with KJ Rose, it was an insightful experience. Her talents, gifts, and her spirit bring the best out of you. As an artist and voice, she possesses that soul and spirit. It was an honor to work and build with her. She is definitely a bright talent."

~ Common, Emmy, Grammy, and Oscar Award-winner, artist, actor, and author

Praises

"KJ Rose is a movement! Her passion for coaching and inspiring people to shine their brightest is contagious and effective."
~ Nikki Buchanan, Director of Multicultural and Audience Segments, Pandora Media

"KJ Rose is a performance coach, faithful teacher, student, confidence cheerleader, and creative curator."
~ Lynn M. Scott, Vice President of Marketing, Hitco Entertainment

"I've watched KJ light up rooms and artists with her energy. And for KJ, that energy is both infectious and teachable. And I appreciate her for putting these gems in a book to share with those artists sitting at home, trying to master their crafts. The Rose Effect is the hammer in your toolbox."
~ Kawan "KP" Prather, Grammy Award-winner, writer, DJ, and executive

"I've had the pleasure of witnessing KJ Rose's tenacity and passion firsthand, as she was determined to tour with Britney Spears, and with my connections and her tenacity, she made it happen. I then watched her pivot into artist development, and I knew that every artist she touched would receive her undeniable skills and explosive energy, thus making them a force on any stage!"
~ Aaron Simon Global Vice President, Talent and Ent Relations, Harman International

"KJ is and always has been a true friend and confidant to the artist. She's the reason the show goes on."
~ Adam Leber, Maverick Management

Praises

"I have watched KJ Rose transition nicely from being a recording artist to working passionately in the space of artist development. There is no one like her."
~ **Marc Beyers, General Manager of Motown Records**

"For a performer to be truly great, they will need inspiration to face their greatest fears. Keanna Henson has perfected 'inspiring herself,' which makes it easy for her to be in the inspiration business. KJ inspires the people who inspire the world."
~**Harold Lilly, CEO Hardcover**

"KJ Rose is more than a coach and artist. She is the performer's performer. Whether it's a speech, a musical, a concert, or a feature film, she brings her best light to help others bring out theirs. The Rose Effect is a must-have for anyone who wants to show up and show out!"
~ **Lynn Richardson, President/COO, MC Lyte's Sunni Gyrl, Inc.**

"KJ defines perfection. A master craftsman in performance, her unique ability to transform an artist's stage presence is remarkable. Taking her guidance, even if you start as a thorn, you'll end up as a ROSE."
~ **John Ehmann, Partner, h.wood media and music executive**

"God just blesses some people, not just with a gift, but with light. KJ is light. And in order to give light to others, you have to possess it yourself. From an artist she's working with to a friend she's

encouraging, she radiates light and love. Anyone who is blessed to receive her gifts has been touched by a powerful force, and they'll never be the same. People like KJ Rose don't grow in bunches like grapes. They are rare like jewels."
~Lamell McMorris, CEO of Phase 2 Consulting

"I have known KJ for over 20 years and have witnessed her growth as an artist and a performance coach firsthand — from seeing her pour her artistic soul out every week at open mics to securing placements as background vocalist on some of the most iconic recordings of the 90s during the apex of the music industry to touring with musical legends, and finally, successfully putting out her own independent album! KJ's fire, energy, and soulfulness enabled her to conquer any challenges that were presented along the way. What I especially loved and witnessed over time was KJ's ability to evolve as an artist and performance professional. Her own self-awareness allowed her to see beyond her own talents and dreams to identify her ability to build out the talents and dreams of others. She is truly the personification of 'to those whom much is given, much is required.' KJ recognized very early on in her journey the impact she has on people and her ability to utilize her energy and performance capabilities to bring out the best in others. She found a way to 'bottle up' the magic she brought to the stage to inspire and enhance the talent of others in search of their own 'fire.' Not only has KJ used this unique skill to benefit artists, but she used the same concepts used to train artists and has expanded them to the corporate boardroom to train and coach business executives to enhance their professional presentation skills through team-building exercises and individual personal development coaching. I don't know many entertainers and entertainment executives who have experienced the same longevity and success as KJ in the ever-changing world of entertainment. Her ability to stay nimble, relevant, and recognize the 'white spaces' where she could make a difference in the world is a true gift. KJ has definitely 'bloomed where she has been planted' and has found success in guiding others to do the same!"

~Erika Munro Kennerly, Global Head of Partnerships and Outreach, Employee Engagement, Google

"KJ's diverse experience in music, combined with passion and unique sensibility, make her amazing to work with! I've been fortunate to witness the development and growth of my artists under her guidance and mentorship. She has a way of helping artists uncover their own magic and take it to the next level."

~ Nicole Plantin, SVP of A&R, Rostrum Records

"Over the years, I have had the pleasure of knowing KJ as a background singer, a solo artist, and a performance coach, and she has always brought a sense of joy, love, and passion to each endeavor. In my humble opinion, she has exactly what is needed to bring out the absolute best in everyone that she works with."

~ Ron Gillyard, entertainment and marketing executive

Praises

"I met KJ in Australia, and she introduced herself by rapping MC Lyte lyrics. That was the point I knew we were friends. In all my years, I'd never come across anyone with the level of intentionality and powerful energy packaged in love like Rose delivers. I wanted to keep her around wherever I went. So, when she told me she wants to deliver that same energy to the masses in book form, I was all in! Oh, and she's FAMUly."
~ Enitan Bereola II, 7x award-winning, 3x bestselling author and marketing executive

"KJ Rose is the light that gives you hope when all you've ever known was darkness. She is a spark that gives your journey meaning."
~ Steve Canal, bestselling author and entrepreneur

"KJ did not just appear! To witness her metamorphosis from talent-show singer to background singer on albums and tours . . . and now teacher and coach is somewhat uncanny. Her levels of belief in her journey have taken a natural progression from a seed to a Rose. Her many years of training have made her an indomitable force! The adjective has not been created to describe her talent, energy, and work ethic, which is unmatched anywhere in the world!"
~Sean Glover, Sound Exchange

"Your hustle is the perfect example of the pivot. When life throws you curve balls you Pivot, adjust and reinvent yourself. Your ability to do that has led you to walk in a different purpose while inspiring and empowering others."
~ Rob Hardy, film director, film producer, screenwriter, and television director

Praises

I've known Keanna K.J. Rose Henson for a very long time. We first met on a rooftop in Harlem both chasing our musical dreams. She was always the brightest spirit with so much life. We always looked forward to seeing her...and now we all look forward to seeing her WIN! I am your friend for life."

~ Anthony Hamilton, Platinum- Selling artist, songwriter, and record producer

FOREWORD

Dynamic! When I think of KJ Rose, dynamic is the first word to come to mind. It describes her perfectly. KJ possesses the most spirited and warm personality. No one cares about her family, friends, and clients like KJ. She is "all in" in the caring department. If you need sage advice, she gives you thought-provoking, kind words at the exact moment you need them— words that encourage you to keep going and striving for a "better way" of life. However, she is no pushover. She is tough when the situation calls for correction and pushes you as close to perfection as possible. She will steer you in the right direction with a stern yet compassionate hand when you teeter on the edge of self-doubt and confidence or are confused about what path to take.

KJ embodies empathy for people in her life. When you are with her, it seems no person or thing matters more to her than you. She feels your pain and your joy; she cries and celebrates with you. She gives you her full attention, and her time is yours. Her compassion is limitless, and her embrace is welcoming.

I have never met a more hardworking and ambitious go-getter than KJ. When she decided to move from New York to LA, I knew she would make a name for herself in a very short time, and she did. KJ

Foreword

does not wait for the world to come to her; she goes out and makes the world her own. That ownership can only happen through hard work and dedication. She was endowed with a wonderful fearless spirit. It took guts to move cross country with the desire to help people reach their maximum potential. She relocated to Los Angeles with a powerful belief system and proficient ability to make a difference in someone's life. She never wavered from her desire to bring out the inner performer of singers, rappers, and corporate executives, to help them improve their performance on stage and in the boardroom. She immediately focuses on you and has an understanding of her client's true life's purpose.

KJ is a giver. Not only does she give as described above, but she has an innate ability to anticipate your needs and help you attain your goals. On any given day, she travels from Santa Monica to the Valley and back to Culver City to work with clients. When she is with them, she does not dwell on her personal stresses. It is never about her; it is about you and what she can do to help elevate your performance, your thoughts, and your spirit.

When I need a lift, I call KJ. I may not always discuss how I feel, but hearing KJ talk about her business and zest for life always makes my spirit soar. She has an infectious personality and is an eternal optimist. She believes in you and knows you can accomplish your aspirations even when you may not see it for yourself yet. She has enough energy and drive for two—until you mirror what she sees in you. When you see it, that is when you begin to open up to new thoughts about yourself, and you blossom.

Once she is in your system, you never want her to go. All her family, friends, and clients can attest to wanting her near and feeling a little melancholy when she goes away. When KJ is around, the atmosphere becomes lighter, brighter, happier, and more fun. You will laugh, get serious, and laugh again. But as lighthearted as KJ can be, she is focused and serious about helping others. She is the perfect friend, counselor, coach, and relative. For me, Keanna is my perfectly dynamic sister.

I love you so much, Keanna. I am bursting with pride as you have accomplished so much in your career. And now I celebrate you as you release *The Rose Effect: Eight Steps to Delivering the Performance of Your Life.* I anticipate this book will continue your mission to help all people perform better, to become more open, free, and as dynamic as you. May the Lord continue to bless you in abundant ways.

Cynthia "CJ" Johnson, music industry executive

FOREWORD II

KJ is not just from Chicago, but the south side of Chicago. This specific side is different from the rest of the city. Great light comes out of darkness, and sometimes the south side is viewed as a dark place; yet so many bright lights shine from this part of the planet.

When I met Keanna, before I even knew her specific talents, I would use a few words to describe what I did see: faith, spirit, love, and energy. In her pursuit as a recording artist, these qualities would carry her through the ups and down of the artist's path. Many people set out to conquer the world through art and music specifically, but few have enough faith, spirit, love, and energy to survive what I sometimes refer to as the "snake pit." The snake pit normally devours all who enter it, regardless of talent or achievements. Most come out of the pit damaged or defeated.

What good is life if you can't help others or find happiness within oneself? As she faced the challenges of her journey, it was in her most vulnerable and difficult times that I witnessed her being prepared for her ultimate calling. Neither of us knew exactly what it would be, but faith is the evidence of the Unseen.

One day, I asked her to take a leap of faith and move from NY to LA. In my eyes, she could only see one step along the staircase, but I knew that God had something for her and all she needed to do was take the first step. Again, it was those four qualities that assured me that her work was God's work. As she emerged from all the dark moments of life, her light began to shine, thus creating *The Rose Effect*.

Dion "No I.D." Wilson, creator, producer, and EVP, Universal Music Group

PREFACE

The round-shaped kitchen table with bright red placemats in my hometown of Chicago has always served as a portal for the best encouragement, heartfelt devotions, and ingenious ideas. This is the table where my family communed and where I found the courage to write.

I also hold New York City responsible for knocking me beyond my perceived capacity. I learned to move with authority and a relentlessness that has shaped me over time. But when I landed in Los Angeles to sing in a film produced by Tri Destined Studios, it was evident that my energy had begun to shift during this visit. LA had reignited my love for performing and the art of performance. I knew it was time to take the leap from a city that had become immensely familiar to one that seemingly offered new possibilities.

I spoke to several individuals who embarked on a similar adventure and could impart a bit of useful insight. One in particular was Devon Franklin, film producer, bestselling author, renowned preacher, and motivational speaker. After reading his book,

Produced by Faith: Enjoy Real Success Without Losing Your True Self, I was sure that a conversation with him would provide the clarity I was seeking. It was my friend Bevy, host, TV personality, and businesswoman, who made it all possible.

I shared with Devon the anguish I was enduring while strategizing this new season of my life. I had so many questions: Do I continue to live in NY and apply for jobs in LA until something becomes available or just move to LA? Devon quickly interjected: "That's not how God works. If he gave you the instructions to move, then you move. We don't get to wait to see how God reveals his hand before we execute. If you are waiting on a YES from anyone else, you are outsourcing your FAITH!"

These words activated my full commitment to expanding my business in Los Angeles. Consequently, I found myself taking client meetings with a stronger posture. I was no longer asking permission to exist; I was now free to be the force that I AM.

But I had still only scratched the surface of my potential. My biggest stretch came from Dustin Felder, actor, acting coach, and motivator, who founded the Dustin Felder Acting Studios and strongly suggested that I create and teach a course at his school. At that moment, it was the worst idea ever, considering I had only worked with singers and thought it best to stay in my lane. He made it clear that my Artist Development and Performance course would be a tool for all performers.

Once I acquiesced, my confidence and stamina became supreme. Before I knew it, I had coached six different classes, six weeks at a time. My armor had become extremely solid every week, and my faith had finally caught up to Dustin's belief in me. Sadly, we lost Dustin, but his impact on my life and so many others will be everlasting.

I began to travel the world, training and conducting workshops for performers of every discipline (singers, actors, executives, dancers, etc.). However, it unnerved me that I was unable to leave them with any tangible resource in which to continue making their transformations. It was evident that I was being challenged to dig deeper, but never had I considered a book. I viewed this type of output as one in which I was declaring that I had arrived. I vacillated between these contrasting thoughts: (1) you haven't done enough to qualify you to write such a book and (2) your desire to help others rediscover their light is what qualifies your call, so fulfill your assignment!

INTRODUCTION

It took me a while to comprehend that I was born for the purpose of being a vessel. It also took a bit of time to accept and connect my identifiable force of "immeasurable energy" to my life's work as an artist development and performance expert. I suppose when my need for external validation diminished, my self-love finally had room to expand. It became easier to make the distinction between merely existing in varying degrees of mediocrity versus abiding in pure joy. Absolute joy is so much better!

I believe that every single person is an artist. Whether you regard yourself as a corporate artist, a creative artist, the quiet or bold artist, you have the right to occupy that space and command your stage. But what happens when talent is evenly distributed to all? How do we leverage our unique value propositions? Do we possess the push-through when our audacity to be remarkable is constantly challenged? Well, I've deduced that it is our ability to deliver and take ownership of our personal stories without compromise that will set us apart.

Before you step onto any stage or into any board-room, audition, write a song, recite a monologue, speak about a product, or most importantly, speak about yourself, you must have an arsenal of landing gear from which to pull and a metric system that tells you when to do so. Uncovering the layers of our own experiences will help us to understand where we can add value, and embracing the vulnerabilities will give us the fuel needed to power through.

The objective of this performance guide is to equip you with the tools required to answer the following questions with a solid measure of certainty: Why you? Would you choose you?

These questions are key to validating and pre-approving yourself rather than outsourcing your point of view. The more you can see yourself, the less you will squander your vision!

Too often we ask permission to exist in our gifts, which garners ambiguity. We can no longer be vague; we must be deliberate.

Talent can be subjective; however, your ability to tell your story in a way that is explicit and compelling is the key to ***Delivering the Performance of Your Life!***

ACKNOWLEDGMENTS

I count you all as my loving crusaders! I have been enriched and strengthened by you. Through the moments of uncertainty, you never let me quit, and you have my sincerest gratitude.

Parents and siblings:
Ma, James, Lamont, and Ashley, I am truly blessed to be an extension of each of you. Ma and James, thank you for consistently having my back, reminding me that I'm never alone and will always have a home to come to. Lamont, you have championed me since we were babies. It was your fire that would often keep my flame going. You are my real MVP. Ashley, one of my goals in life is to be a pillar of strength and an example of resilience for you, I hope I have made you proud. Love you all.

Aunts, uncles, cousins, grandparents, godchildren, godmother and ancestors:
I stand taller because of you. You are my rocks! Thank you for your light.

Granddaddy:
You are the greatest example of hard work, success, and absolute humor. You bring me so much joy. Thank you for loving me.

Acknowledgments

FamuBFFs + Fellas:
Thank you for your friendship and your prayers. You have carried me more than you can imagine. I also firmly believe that the heavenly guidance of our ladybug, Leslie Nicole Clarke Gregg, has lifted my spirit. We love you, Taylor!

Sorors, BADST, and the Telluric 41 of the Majestic Majesty:
All of my love forever. Delta Sigma Theta Sorority, Inc., thank you.

FAMUly:
We are bonded by the hills forever. Thank you.

Emmanuelites:
Your heart and your love has shaped me. Thank you.

Tri Destined Studios family:
You have cheered, prayed, and loved on me . . . and it has all counted. Thank you.

Camp Cuties:
Thank you for the many adventures and conversations that have emboldened me every second. You have loved me through every season.

Chateau Parnell:
Thank you, Motisola Zulu and Adrienne Alexander, for providing me the space and encouragement to build upon my ideas. I appreciate all of you ladies — Michelle Huff, Beny Ashburn, and Kiki Kitty.

Acknowledgments

Coaches:
A coach needs a coach! Thank you Craig Derry, Clurel Henderson, and Milton Jones.

Dope friends (around the world):
This win was inevitable with you by my side. Thank you.

Hustle Her Squad:
As my fellow artists, I'm so grateful that we *truly GET* each other. You ladies inspire me to keep going! Thank you for everything.

Crazy broads and a Cool dude:
Where would I be without you? I never want to find out. Love you all for the truth and the humor.

NYC RF crew:
Thank you for always being there, from the choreography in the living room to full-out dancing on stage! I appreciate you!

Music Managers:
Your guidance gave me the strength to push through on so many days. Thank you Dave Nelson, Erskine Issac, Datu Faison, and Rick Brown.

Pastors and Spiritual advisors:
Thank you for feeding my soul with the Word and preparing me to be a vessel for the world. I will continue to give God the glory at all times.

Dr. Lester W. Taylor and Gayle Taylor *Community Baptist Church - Englewood, NJ*

Acknowledgments

Warryn Campbell and Erica Campbell *California Worship Center - North Hollywood, CA*

Devon Franklin and Meagan Good

Eddie Samuel Sheffield and LaTrina Sheffield

Marshall Mitchell

Attorneys: Your friendship and expertise has been invaluable to me through the years, Matt Middleton and James McMillian.

The Rose Effect Creative Team: Myra Barrera, Johnnie Tangle, Ebonie Marie, Oriny Dera, Hope Rippere, Carl Weber, Martha Weber, Walter Nixon and Matt Jong. Your creative layups have been essential and necessary to completing this task. Thank you.

SaintMiles Agency and Marketing team:
You are the ultimate motivators. I'm grateful for your patience, expertise, and faith in me. Thank you, Steve Canal and Enitan Bereola, for making sure the world received this book.

Entertainment industry mentors:
I soar because you believed and pushed me. Thank you, Sean Glover, Cynthia Johnson, and Dion "NO I.D." Wilson, Jon Platt, Dave Nelson, and Erskine Isaac.

Board of Directors:
I'm so much wiser because of your golden, give-it-to-me-straight advice and support. Thank you,

Acknowledgments

Ghian Foreman, Lamell McMorris, Marc Beyers, Sean Glover, and Dave Fuller.

To Everyone That Has Championed Me On My First Album, "All Heart, No Regrets":
Thank you for showing me so much love on this album. This truly gave me the burst of confidence I needed to tour the country and share my music. *PRODUCERS:* Jax, No I.D., Extreme, Andy C., Dwayne Bastiany, Harvy AllBangers, Rhymefest, Terry Hunter, Jermaine Mobley and Jordan Battiste.

To The Artists Who Have Trusted Me With Their Gifts:
It has been an honor to serve you. You have stretched me more than you know. I love you all. Thank you.

To Those Who Have Contributed To My Story:
You have blessed me and poured into me. You will forever be a part of my life's journey. Thank you.

To Every Person Who Has Blessed Me With A Testimonial:
The depth of your words and fullness of your hearts are a reminder that God has always had me covered. Thank you, Jax, Lil Nas X, Nikaya D. Brown Jones, Phylicia Fant, No I.D., Cynthia Johnson, Steve Pamon, Shawn Holiday, Erica Campbell, Common, Nikki Buchanan, Marc Beyers, Ron Gilliard, Aaron Simon, Gee Roberson, Adam Leber, Lynne M. Scott, Nicole Plantin, Lamell McMorris, Lynn Richardson, Harold Lilly, John Ehmann, Erika Munro, Enitan Bereola II, Steve Canal, Sean Glover, Rob Hardy and Anthony Hamilton.

CONTENTS

Destined to Bloom

My mother and father named me Keanna Rose Henson. It wasn't until I was older that I fully grasped how deeply the *Rose* was planted.

My mother's middle name is **Rosa**.

My maternal grandmother's name was **Rosa**.

My maternal great-great grandmother's name was **Rosa**.

My paternal grandmother's name was **Rose**.

As much as I tried to dismiss the *Rose*, complaining that it made me appear older, it was inescapable, and would take years to recognize the *courage* rooted in the name.

While pursuing a career in music, I thought it would be best to go with the stage name Keanna, as it made the most sense. But after I began touring with several artists as a background vocalist, it was tough for some music executives to see me in the foreground as a solo artist. I'd walk into record label meetings to discuss my music, and they would almost instantly say, "Oh, you're Keanna, the backup singer." It felt so defeating. Although my background work was an important part of my journey, I now endeavored to be seen through a new lens, and I would need to reset the perception that standing in the back was my only option.

The disappointing outcome of these meetings led me toward a deeper appreciation for my lineage, the *Rose*. I didn't realize how impactful this rediscovery would be. I was desperate to break out of the box people were trying to place me in, and even if they perceived me as an unknown new artist for ten minutes, it was still better than being relegated to the dim lights. But it wouldn't be long before KJ Rose was born, and she was *beyond courageous*!

Now, I'm sure you're wondering what the *J* stands for, so let me explain. At a point in time, I was married and took on his last name of Johnson. By the time the marriage dissolved, the name KJ Rose had begun to take off, and I refused to look back. It was clear that in order for me to find peace in this, I had to completely reassign the *J* — so Johnson was OUT, and *Joyful, Jesus Saves,* and *Jubilee* was IN. Take your pick!

She surrendered; she Rose.

The Rose Effect...

CHAPTER 1

THE APOLLO,
THE APPLAUSE

Applause: approval or praise expressed by clapping

I possessed a stage fright that was unusual and debilitating at times. I was able to dance, cheer, and thrive comfortably in crowds, but the minute I was asked to deliver a speech or sing a solo, a temporary sickness would instantly consume my body. I would get this feeling of nausea as if I were on the floor-drop ride at the amusement park. It was difficult to resolve my passion for music while singing with the presence of such trepidation.

This adverse reaction continued for years, even triggering my mother to question if this was the career choice I should be attempting. My mom is one of my biggest supporters, though she was quite partial to me working in Corporate America. The more pragmatic choice lessened her worry. However, she made a great point, and I thought it best to counter this reaction by throwing myself into the New York open mic scene, where vocalists would go to showcase their talent with a live band and phenomenal hosts like the late Ron Grant. I booked countless recording sessions and vocal lessons with my notable coach, Craig Derry. Craig's belief in my abilities at times outweighed my own. I tried my best to perform with ease like my Chicago friend and Bad Boy's R&B crooner, Carl Thomas, but I could never quite measure up to his level of cool. However, he was the first to take me on tour to help me get more training.

Additionally, my brother and I formed a group named JaxsonRose, and while it brought me great comfort to have him on stage with me, my spirit was still quite unsettled, and I stepped away from it. This is something I still regret.

I was determined to shock my system into creating the space for my nerves and my desire to perform to co-exist. So, I took a heck of a leap and thrust myself into what many would call the lion's den, depending on your outlook. Yes, the world-famous *Showtime at the Apollo!* With the encouragement of my management team, Dave and Erskine, I nervously forged ahead.

For my very first performance on this stage, I sang Anita Baker's "Sweet Love," and to my surprise, your girl did her thang and won! This was a good sign. I received thunderous applause from the audience, and it appeared that I was on my way to combating my stage fright.

I was determined to shock my system into creating the space for my nerves and my desire to perform to co-exist.

The following month, they brought back the past winners for an All-Stars competition. I was feeling a bit sick beforehand, but at least I knew what to expect this time. I sang another Anita Baker song, and the familiarity of the applause once again gave me the comfort I so desperately needed. At the end of the show, they brought out all the contestants, and the audience had to show their love by applauding those they enjoyed or booing those they did not. For clarity, there were some people that barely made it through their initial performances without a slight crescendo of disapproval from the audience; however, they at least received a nod of kind recognition and soft applause during the judging process.

I stood on stage in the seventh position, which left only one performer after me. Now, this performer had a very nice voice and traveled from Maryland to compete with fifty of her biggest cheerleaders in tow. As I'm sure you can gather by now, when it came time for the audience to decide my fate, her entire pep squad booed me, while instantly cheering for her! It was painfully clear that she was the winner. Fighting back tears, I smiled and graciously congratulated her while crumbling inside.

Bowlegged Lou, artist, producer, and member of the epic group Full Force, was the host that evening. He challenged the audience on my behalf and then turned to me and said, "This is entertainment, baby. You better keep singing and don't ever give up!" All the applause had ceased, and I now had to decide if the embarrassment and excruciating feeling of defeat would cause me to give up or push through. But I could not put my future in the hands of people who were uninformed of my potential. I had to forge ahead.

Our belief cannot waiver! We must pre-approve ourselves before seeking the approval of others. Neither the applause nor the boos can define our mission. Wherever you occupy space, that is your stage, and you must command it wholeheartedly.

The applause will never determine your *Yes*. You have already been qualified. You are the *Yes!*

THE BLOOM

Share an experience when you truly felt defeated or undervalued while trying to fulfill your purpose.

_____

_____

_____

_____

Share some ways in which it made you better:

_____

_____

_____

_____

CHAPTER 2

Sorry, It's Not Personal

To take it PERSONALLY: to get upset by the things other people say or do because you think that their remarks or behavior are directed at you in particular

I've been beyond fortunate as a background vocalist to work with a few recording artists that include P. Diddy, Britney Spears, Justin Timberlake, Janet Jackson, Notorious B.I.G., Common, KRS1, Mase, Carl Thomas, Jax, dead prez, BSTC, Sean Lett, Malik Yusef, Monica, Rhymefest, and several others. These artists pushed me to be better, but there was another who surely changed my life.

Late one evening, I received a call from my manager, Dave Nelson, that would shift my trajectory as a vocalist. He asked if I could rush to the studio to lay vocals for Tony Dofat, multi-platinum producer and composer, DJ, associate professor, and a member of The Hit Men. It was about 11 PM, and I immediately called a car service from Brooklyn to 57th Street in Manhattan. When I arrived, I could not believe that I would be working with the incomparable and lovable Heavy D, a Grammy Award–winning rapper, producer, singer, and actor!

Most of the calls I received to sing started out as the producer merely needing an extra voice, any voice . . . but I was aware that my presence was not a coincidence. I knew they were looking for me, and my job was to show up every single time. Showing up will take you to levels you never imagined.

The lyrics had already been prepared, so I recorded my part upon Hev's and Tony's direction. I was done at about 2 AM, and I proceeded back to Brooklyn to get a little rest before heading to work at Pfizer Pharmaceuticals at 8 AM. Days later, I was notified by Dave and Deo (the Universal Records A&R rep) that Hev and the label loved the song and were planning to make it a single on his *Waterbed*

Hev album. This song was entitled "Big Daddy," and it would become my very first credit as a professional vocalist.

There is no feeling quite like the one that permeated my spirit as my friend and sorority sister Nikaya, Dave, and I drove down the Westside Highway in New York City, listening to my voice on Hot 97, the number-one hip-hop radio station in New York. We bumped my song "Big Daddy" as loud as we could while I hung out of the window, screaming the lyrics with sheer elation. It was finally my moment, and it was surreal.

I was invited to be in the video by one of the label executives. I was grateful for this opportunity, but the only caveat was that it was taking place in Los Angeles and I would be responsible for my travel and accommodations. I didn't give this a second thought. We booked the flights, and we were out!

Just to give you a little bit of background: I met my managers Dave and Erskine through a friend, Big Jon Platt, Chairman and CEO of Sony/ATV Music Publishing. Jon and I met through our mutual friend and my sorority sister Shelly, when he attended her college graduation at FAMU during the time he worked at EMI Music Publishing. As I sat atop the stairs and Jon stood at the base, my friends encouraged me to sing for him. I was initially very shy, but once he announced that he would be leaving the next morning, I belted out a tune, and he subsequently introduced me to his friends, who would become my managers.

When Dave and I arrived in Los Angeles, Big Jon was the person who graciously accommodated us. It was my first time ever in Hollywood, and I was so anxious to be a part of my very first video feature.

I could barely sleep! We woke up the next morning to rain, but my spirits were high, as I was soon to embark on the performance of a lifetime.

We ventured onto the Universal lot and were escorted to the appropriate stage. I proudly announced that I was the talent for the video shoot; however, no one seemed to be expecting my arrival. A few people tried to assist, but I was eventually told there was no place for me in the video. I lamented that I was the girl who sang on the hook, but it didn't change anything, and I was turned away. I could see inside as the dancers were stretching and were preparing to film the video, while I just stood there teary-eyed and practically begging to be included.

I thought this was the meanest joke ever played, but I would later learn that none of this was a joke nor actually about me. There seemed to be a bit of discourse between a few of the executives, and I had become a casualty of that exchange. It felt so personal. This would serve as another one of my greatest disappointments. The excitement that once existed for this voyage had swiftly come to a complete halt, and we were left with no choice but to head back to New York. My heart was bruised, the money had been spent, and I had nothing to show for it.

I could see inside as the dancers were stretching and preparing to film, while I stood teary-eyed and practically begging to be included.

I was angry, sad, disappointed, defeated, and any other less-than-joyful emotion you can think of. After a few weeks of this utter misery, I received a call from the label requesting my vocals on the remix of "Big Daddy." Some nerve, right? I'm sure you can imagine my initial response to this request. Yep, I said hell nawl! Fool me once, shame on you, but fool me twice . . . No, thank you, sir.

Well, I'm not that crazy, and most of this sarcasm and sass took place only in my head! Once I regained my center and operated in my highest level of consciousness, I realized that I was standing in the middle of bonus territory. I could now seize another opportunity or potentially miss one. It appeared my vocals had become part of the formula that led to the success of the single.

The harsh reality was that nobody owed me anything. Every inch, every *yes*, every *maybe*, every door, and every opportunity was a blessing.

There was no place for my ego. This was merely business, and my feelings were not invited. Secondly, the alternative was less appealing. They could have called another singer, and I would have just been a singer of the past. I didn't want to give up a chance for the world to hear my voice for a second time!

I believe it was this mindset that would guide me to the next epic and platinum project, *Life After Death*, Notorious B.I.G.'s album produced by P. Diddy and Stevie J. It was Deric "D-Dot" Angelettie aka The Mad Rapper, producer, and member of The Hit Men, who hired me for this project. These experiences blew my mind, as I found myself moving amongst artists who shifted the culture of hip-hop.

I tried my hardest to return to the studio with my serious/I'm-not-your-friend game face on while pushing aside my feelings, focusing on the work, but Hev's energy completely changed my stoic presence. I believe he felt slightly bad about the circumstances surrounding the video, which made him unbelievably kind and jovial.

I truly felt his sincerity, but of course, there was still a petty part of me that hoped for the perfect moment to share my thoughts on the way I was treated. Well, the opportunity to repair my bruised ego would come sooner than I expected.

Months later, I was partying with my girls, and Hev was a bit smitten with my friend Erika, so he asked me to introduce him and relay what an awesome guy he was. So, I eagerly announced, "Well, as long as you are not interested in being in Hev's music video, he's a great guy!" After the initial shock, everyone erupted into laughter, and I finally had my sweet vindication and enjoyed every second of it! Hev chuckled and took it in stride, and now our friendship could truly begin.

It was because of Tony, Hev, Dave, Erskine, and Deo that my family could now see my work in New York was paying off and my grandfather could finally stop asking, "Now, what are your goals in life, baby?" Hev and I continued to work together, and he consistently encouraged me to leap outside of my comfort zone. I will forever be grateful to Hev for these enriching experiences. I am so much stronger because of them.

Rest in Heaven, Dave Nelson and Dwight "Heavy D" Myers.

I've collected more wins by merely showing up. Half of the battle is showing up. While in pursuit of our dreams, it's imperative that we quickly resolve the negative emotions we may feel when faced with rejection.

Our ego should be used as a healthy metric system for assessing when to move forward with potential opportunities. But we may often find ourselves making an emotionally-charged decision if our ego is not managed properly.

THE BLOOM

I nearly missed a chance to build both my career and a relationship with Hev because I felt slighted after being excluded from the video. This provided a teachable moment of humility.

1. Share a few instances when you've felt dismissed and then share your response to each of them.

   _____

   _____

   _____

2. If you could retrace your steps, what are some ways in which you could have responded or handled it differently?

   _____

   _____

   _____

CHAPTER 3

Is It Ever Really Defeat?

Defeat: failure to succeed or to win

Performance is merely an outward expression of what you believe about yourself. Therefore, the time you spend collecting information and doing the internal work is crucial.

By day, I was recording my music. By night, I was an evening receptionist at J Records. After a few months, I was asked to work directly for Clive Davis, record producer, author, and A&R and music executive, as one of his executive assistants. As you can imagine, this was certainly a daunting request. My sis, CJ, who had been my mentor since the beginning of time, was a huge advocate for this new role. She was the first woman I saw dominating the music industry as SVP of Radio Promotions, blazing trails and making epic strides. CJ had to walk me through this process because my initial response was, "No, thank you." After further deliberation, I realized that this would not only provide an invaluable education in the music industry, but it would refine my overall business acumen. I accepted the offer.

It was quite intimidating to work with the iconic figure who was responsible for the careers of such legends as Whitney Houston, Aretha Franklin, Carlos Santana, Jennifer Hudson, Alicia Keys, and so many others. I prepared myself with a level of impenetrable confidence every time I would need to open the heavy burgundy doors to receive his next request. We began to develop a soft rapport throughout the years. It took everything in me not to scream that I was a singer who had traveled the world with some of the greatest artists, but I ultimately decided it would be a wildly short-sighted approach to informing him of my talent. Therefore, I stayed the course and did my best at the job I was hired to do, while quietly working and hoping that my presence would eventually open some new doors. My days were filled with humbling tasks and insightful observations. I decided that for every message recorded, trip booked, or meeting scheduled, I would somehow initiate a music-related conversation with Mr. Davis. I would ask questions like: *Why did you choose that as a single? What do you like about this record?* My thought process was that I needed to find a way for this to be a win-win exchange for us both. This could only happen with a healthy attitude and a mission to deliver every request with excellence.

Interacting with Mr. Davis taught me how to project my voice and opinion both concisely and deliberately. My goal was to remain inquisitive when I set foot in the building. With every encounter, I grew increasingly emboldened by more of these "teachable moments." They fueled me to walk onto any stage and into any room with an unwavering measure of presence.

Clive Davis had become my mentor. I admired his work ethic, as he never rested upon his previous laurels nor settled for anything mediocre. Mr. Davis' drive to efficiently serve his artists in every facet of their career was motivating. My proximity to this eco-system had given me a proverbial front-row seat to the inner workings of a label and its players.

During my lunch breaks, I would sit with A&R executives Larry and John, who would listen to my songs and offer very sound feedback. Their encouragement was so critical. I yearned deeply for a record deal, but between the politics and the timing, it seemed unattainable. This felt like another effort of futility.

My days were filled with humbling tasks yet substantial teaching moments. They fueled me to walk onto any stage and into any room with an unwavering measure of presence.

As the learning curve began to diminish, it was time to assess my tangible options. I thought it best to continue cultivating my skills as a performer, and I accepted a job with a promotional tour as a background vocalist. The irony was that Mr. Davis had no idea I could even sing, so giving him a resignation letter stating that I would be leaving my post as his assistant to tour with Janet Jackson was quite shocking, I'm sure. The following day, I arrived at the office and with the support of my girls Paula and Deana, who were the highly skilled women behind the Chairman (Mr. Davis) and the COO (Charles Goldstuck), I walked into Mr. Davis' office to offer him some ice tea and possibly receive his response to my letter.

Although he was in a meeting with a few executives, he erupted with excitement, yelling, "Does everyone know where Keanna is headed? She's going to dance with Janet Jackson!"

I gently corrected him. "I'm going to sing."

He said, "Yes, to sing with Janet!"

I was slightly stunned by this enthusiasm, as it belied our past reserved exchanges, but the acknowledgment truly warmed my heart. Although I never left with the record deal I was seeking, I did walk away with a relationship with Mr. Davis, great friends from J Records, wisdom, and a jolt of renewed energy.

A year later, I completed my music single entitled "A Better Way," and asked Mr. Davis to review it. He was quite candid and expressed that he didn't hear this as a suitable radio hit, but I still counted this as a win because he took the time to listen and because I had finished the task. This was a full-circle experience that would enrich and contribute to the rest of my journey as a performer and a coach. I left J Records with the readiness and confidence to take on the world.

While some encounters are meant to garner the exact results we seek, there are also those that don't quite measure up to our expectations. Those are the encounters meant to shape us and set us up for the opportunities we don't see coming. We must embrace them, keep pushing, and seeking ways to hone and intensify our skills.

THE BLOOM

What are a few things that you can do to improve as a person and become more skilled in your craft?

1. _____

_____

_____

2. _____

_____

_____

3. _____

_____

_____

Start today!

CHAPTER 4

Pivot and Prevail

Pivot: to turn or rotate

Ibecame so accustomed to the *chasing* and the *laboring* of accomplishing my dreams that I neglected to take the time to distinguish how much of it was pointless activity versus viable productivity. I found myself on autopilot, totally unaware that I might have been running the wrong race. At times, I was so afraid of *being still* that it felt better to keep running, even if it was in the wrong direction. For some odd reason, movement equaled progress for me. I had begun to allow the emotional and physical fatigue to become the metric system for tracking my success.

Sometimes we are afraid to stop and assess our progress because it might require us to pivot and head toward a new direction. The idea of making a pivot can be difficult, based on our perspectives. Pivoting might garner a feeling of regret for the time we think we've wasted in the wrong direction, but it also provides us with valuable insight into the right course. Time is never lost; it might just count toward something greater. When we neglect to take stock of our progress or lack thereof, we tend to find ourselves in places by default. Whenever I have felt regret, it's because I've allowed ambivalence to direct me instead of making a deliberate choice.

I've written songs for years, spent over 10,000+ hours in studios, performed at many venues honing my skills, planting seeds, and going to vocal classes, but there were many times that I felt I wasn't good enough and even questioned if I truly had a gift. While I enjoyed creating music, how dare I try to make a career of it? The sacrifices surely outweighed the rewards, and there was no sign of winning. I had endured a divorce, missed important bonding moments with my family and friends. I opted out of most group dinners and celebrations because ordering an appetizer never seemed to cut it, and computing the check after the meal gave me anxiety. I was always one meager paycheck away from retreating back home to Chicago and unsure how much longer I could endure it all. These sacrifices were supposed to add up to stardom and a record deal, but that deal never came. I was now left trying to reconcile it all. Had I been defeated, or had a portion of my assignment come to a close?

Whenever I have felt regret, it's because I've allowed ambivalence to direct me instead of making a deliberate choice.

While trying to resolve this new space, I landed a few roles at AMC Networks (Sundance TV/ IFC) in original programming/sales. These jobs were intended to be temporary assignments, but they quickly became permanent positions, as I found myself working there for six years. There were days I felt very stagnant and unseen, but my need for clarity and financial stability provided another necessary pivot. It appeared that I was back on my corporate grind, running to catch a bus from New Jersey, galloping to catch the A train to Midtown, bobbing and weaving through the uncomfortably crowded Penn Station, and sweating profusely by the time I reached my desk. But somehow, it was all worth it.

My need to prove that I was more than just their assistant caused me to be very vocal about my music background. To my surprise, my talents were celebrated and utilized in some of the Sundance

TV series and branded entertainment spots. I even got to perform at the Sundance Film Festival in Park City, Utah. This pivot offered me a broader scope of the entertainment industry, as my view had been a very narrow one. I found myself developing new skill sets in an unexpected place.

There was a freedom in this new place that no corporate job had offered before. Working in this office allowed me access to talented people in every single department, which I fully utilized to create my solo album, "All Heart, No Regrets." Yvette worked for Sarah, the president, but she was also a stylist and seamstress; Kelli was a marketing manager; Cassandra was in affiliate marketing, and Jessie was also a singer. They shared all of their gifts with me. There was so much talent all around me, from the leadership (Josh, Ed, and Charlie) to my direct managers and co-workers. By honoring my current space at AMC Networks, my vision and next chapter had come to life. I must remind you that I had considered my roles at Sundance/ IFC to be limited and temporary, but God had a greater plan, and it was so much better!

I now had the confidence to put out an album and perform throughout the country. It had taken me ten years to believe that I was good enough to be an artist. Working toward this goal had been a familiar pursuit, and I had finally completed the task.

After a few months of fully operating in what I thought I wanted, my desire to continue as a vocal artist had diminished. In a strange way, I had grown dependent on the struggle because it validated the sacrifices. Could shifting gears prove the doubters correct? Was I not built for this? Or could I have been the greatest doubter of them all? This train of thought was very unhealthy and required a lot of prayer and internal validation. I had to release myself from believing another route might have been better. I needed to accept that I was exactly where I was meant to be in order to share this very specific testimony.

While I believed my career was an essential part of my trajectory, it was becoming clear that there were still more layers to uncover. I was later asked by Carolyn at J Records to help a few of the artists with their stage presence, but it was imperative that I accepted this new challenge by choice and not by default. Once I understood that it was truly a natural progression for my career, I could wholeheartedly embrace it.

I remember someone asking, "Why didn't you make it as a singer? You're really good at what you do." That question sent piercing waves through my body as I wondered if I had given up. But after coming back to my senses, I recognized that my singing career (the talent) would reveal my true calling as a coach (the assignment). The next time someone made a similar statement, my response would be, "I did make it. You just missed it." It felt so refreshing to say, and even better to believe it! I would no longer allow others to box me in or define my career, as it is continuously expanding.

People often advise us based on their own personal fears or limiting thoughts, but somehow, we internalize them. This is where it stops. Pivots don't discount the work you've already done, but they add more depth and richness to your vision. They give you the armor to sustain in moments of doubt; they give range; they provide a foundation and set you up for your next assignment!

THE BLOOM

While working toward our goals, we must take a moment to examine our process.
What areas of your pursuit seem to be working?

_____

_____

_____

What are the results that represent your progress?

_____

_____

_____

Identify the areas in which you may need to adjust or pivot.

_____

_____

_____

CHAPTER 5

From Shame to Significance

Shame: a painful feeling of humiliation or distress caused by the consciousness of wrong or foolish behavior

Shame may often keep you in places that no longer serve you. That place for me happened to be a failed marriage. As a hopeless romantic, I truly believed in my happily ever after. It's what I prayed for. However, I partnered with someone who lacked the capacity to see the fullness of my heart. While I was deep into planning my wedding, there was another woman deep into planning to deliver my fiancé's child. To be fair, we were not together upon their encounter, but we were together when he was made aware of her pregnancy. He concealed this information for years, and it was clear the marriage never stood a chance. I was informed of this due to a *misdirected* Father's Day card from his son that was mailed to my home during our separation.

Anything built on faulty ground cannot be sustained. Ironically, the birth of his son was not what directly ended the marriage. The marriage dissolved because of the immense insecurity, shame, and coldness that grew from the ongoing deceit of the concealment of his child. The projection of this toxicity caused me to question my own confidence. Before his secret was revealed, I was left to my own devices to figure out why his definition of love didn't seem to coincide with mine. To cope, I threw myself into my music. I thought if I could just become a successful artist (i.e., financially stable), then he would be kinder. I had no idea that his behavior was compounded with layers of emotional baggage. A partner is meant to add value, elevate, champion, and love you unconditionally. Somewhere, we fell short.

When going through heartache, it's difficult to embrace the notion that God will take your most painful moments and use them for his good. During this time, I yearned for an emotional escape, which led me to write a song called "A Better Way." It was a personal declaration and reminder that I was never meant for mediocrity. Throughout the years, women have shared that this song empowered them to make better choices, though it would also immediately transport me back to a place of sadness.

Shame may often keep you in places that no longer serve you.

Years later, my friend Rochelle introduced me to Shannon, a phenomenal editor and music consultant, who inquired if I might have any original music I could submit to a project she was overseeing. My initial response was, "I got nothing." Rochelle challenged my statement as she reminded me of the album I had recorded. In this moment, I was thinking that I had evolved as a writer and could possibly submit something that was more current. But she had no time for my evolution; she needed it asap. So, I took a chance and submitted the song that I had written nine years ago, "A Better Way."

It was a personal declaration and reminder that I was never meant for mediocrity.

A month later, in an episode of the OWN (Oprah Winfrey Network) television series *Queen Sugar*, "A Better Way" served as the sentimental backdrop to one of the most gripping scenes between the characters Aunt Vi and Hollywood. To hear the words that had been written from a dark space of shame, discouragement, and hopelessness now repurposed to tell a story of unconditional love, commitment, and honor was soul-stirring. I quickly realized a few things: God can redeem time and take something that we disqualify as old and make it new again. Within 52 seconds, the duration of the scene, my attachment to this song had been beautifully redefined.

Don't let any thought, idea, or body of work that you believe in go to waste. Write it down, take a break, revisit it, and then finish it. We disqualify ourselves from great opportunities because we believe it's our job to figure out where it will land or how it will be perceived. However, our only job is to honor the art, honor the work, and detach ourselves from the end results. We must trust that it will land safely.

THE BLOOM

Name 5 projects (song, poem, script, dance, monologue, thesis, idea . . . anything) that you have left incomplete.

1. _____

_____

2. _____

_____

3. _____

_____

4. _____

_____

5. _____

_____

NOW CHOOSE ONE TO COMPLETE!

CHAPTER 6

Don't Let the Bright Lights Blind You

Bright (lights): giving out or reflecting a lot of light; shining

New York took me on the ride of a lifetime. Upon graduating from FAMU in Tallahassee, FL, I was ready to take on the concrete jungle of NYC. I was blessed with friends who were NY natives like Shane, Salima, and Marilyn (Carolyn), who helped me to navigate the Big Apple a lot more easily than I could have on my own. These ladies happened to be the talented dancers behind our beloved Whitney Houston and Bobby Brown, and their energy was comparable to mine. There were days I would find myself standing in the middle of Times Square, observing the people and looking up at the tall buildings, like many of the curious tourists. Eventually, I found myself moving at a quicker pace and being annoyed by the tourists who couldn't help but look up as well! When you can't stand the tourist activity you once participated in, you are an official New Yorker.

I had survived the brutal snowstorms and countless sprints down the staircases to catch the subway, the late-night studio sessions and open mics, the epic Chuck Bone & Wendall industry parties, and record label meetings in hopes that one conversation might change the course of my life. I stomached the quick naps in the restroom throughout the day at my corporate job and loads of empty auditions. It was inevitable that I would develop an impenetrable armor and relentless spirit. At this point, the weight of the word *No* meant very little to me because I was programmed to work until I was presented with a tangible *Yes*.

When I moved to the West Coast, I disagreed with those who suggested that Hollywood would require different energy, but I was quickly humbled. There was a prestigious yearly luncheon for women in the entertainment industry who were defined as the consummate game-changers. This was a highly coveted event, and although I never received an invitation, it was beyond aspirational. Now, this was the year that Oprah Winfrey would be speaking, so my sense of urgency was incredibly high! I was determined to be in the room.

My friend Anthea had come into town with the same audacious goal in mind, so we dressed up and forged ahead to the Beverly Hills Hotel. We strolled up to the check-in desk with immense confidence. I boldly gave my name as if I were on the list. Clearly, they were unable to locate KJ Rose, but I stayed the course by giving the young lady every moniker I could think of (Keanna Henson, Keanna Rose, K. Rose, etc.) in hopes that she would become exhausted and empathetic. Sadly, she never did.

I waited off to the side, praying I would see someone that could help, but the time waiting had slowly revealed desperation—and this eventually became embarrassing. My ego could no longer take it. It was uncomfortable watching my peers walk in with such boldness, knowing they were invited guests. Once again, I was on the outside, peering in. Yes, it was merely a party, but as a dreamer, I was constantly in search of one new contact, a conversation, information, or inspiration that I could hold onto. Anything that could convince me that moving to Los Angeles was the right move.

We were turned away, feeling defeated, and proceeded to lunch while lamenting the fact that we were not included. I called my mom and shared what had occurred.

Her response was simple. "Well, I don't quite understand why you're so upset considering the fact you were never on the list."

I responded, "Well, Mom, this is not the time to make sense, and maybe you and I have not met properly. I have encountered more wins than losses, but today was definitely a loss." I constantly shock my mom with some of my decisions because she's a lot more conservative than I am. Yet she's my biggest prayer warrior!

The following day, I was invited to a vocal boot camp by Mindy and Raab, my friends who happen to be celebrity vocal experts. They wanted to introduce me to other vocal coaches, but I was hesitant to make the two-hour drive. Additionally, I was still consumed with bitterness over not being able to see Oprah.

I had a conversation with my dear friend, Nikaya, who said, "I just don't understand why you are focusing so hard on the shiny door that has closed versus the not-so-shiny door that is wide open and welcoming."

Initially, I was defensive; however, after giving it some thought, I understood that she was absolutely correct. Though it wasn't a red-carpet affair, they were excited to have me. I made the decision to attend the camp in San Bernardino, where I was introduced to loads of talented teachers, coaches, and singers. I took about twenty business cards and returned home empty-handed. This particular *Yes* to attending the camp, jumpstarted my business as an artist performance expert in Los Angeles. I had nearly missed this moment of opportunity as I was focused on yesterday's disappointment. This taught me to recover quicker.

While driving back from the camp, I received a call to attend a pre-Oscar party. This was special because it was hosted by Chicago's very own Oscar-winning rapper and actor, Common. As I walked into the dimly lit room full of ambiance, I realized that a private dinner preceded the party, and I found myself standing a few feet away from Oprah, Shonda Rhimes, David Oyelowo, and Tyrese Gibson. They were dancing with one another. Just a few days earlier, I had been disheartened to be left out of the room with hundreds to see Oprah, and now I was in an intimate space within arm's length of her. I immediately understood the lesson in this. God was saying:

"Stop trying to force entry into doors that I never gave you access to because the ones I have for you, I will open!"

I was excited to share all of my hopes, dreams, and aspirations with Oprah, but my spirit told me to yield. I proceeded to a corner away from the crowd to ask God, "If not now, then when?"

All I got in return was, "In due time." I politely requested a photo with Oprah, and she was gracious enough to oblige. I snapped the shot and begrudgingly walked away.

The following day, I received a call from Vanessa and Alan, my former bosses from IFC/AMC networks, who invited me to attend the Independent Spirit Awards in Santa Monica the following weekend. My friend Nikaya and I were delighted to be in this room. We were located at Table 75, and my former bosses were at Table 2 when I received a text that read: Oprah has just entered the side door, and she is at Table 1! They were also aware of my Lady O plight. Now, this was all a bit surreal. Who sees

Oprah twice in a week? Nikaya and I declared: *it's time to be bold!*

There were only a few minutes allotted to walking during the commercial breaks, and I was approximately 73 tables away from completing the mission. So, I started walking and made it about halfway—but then I punked out and scurried back to my seat.

But then I said, "Keanna, get yourself together. There are no coincidences. This is bigger than you. You are a vessel; you are of His greatness and nothing less!" I needed to light my internal fire and instantly create a personal power chant before my second attempt.

I proceeded to walk over during the next break only to encounter the security guard who was standing in front of Lady O. As I got closer, he put his arm out to guard the space.

I politely tapped it, saying, "Don't worry about it. I just gotta do something." I swiftly walked around Oprah's table to my former bosses at Table 2 to greet them. I finally sashayed behind the security guard, greeted Ava Duvernay, and knelt beside Oprah (she was eating bread). I introduced myself, explaining that we had taken a cute picture at Common's party just days before, and I thought she might want to see it. Mentioning his party instantly vetted me and made my introduction appear less arbitrary.

"Sure," she said, so I swiped to the photo, and she responded. "It *is* cute!"

Then I delivered my fifteen-second pitch, gave her my business card, and stated, "If there are any opportunities in which I could add value to you as an artist performance expert, I would be honored if you would consider me."

She took my card, checked out the front and back, and responded with a zestful "Okay!"

Victory was mine in this moment! The mission was complete, and I got the heck out of there before her security guard put me in a headlock. This was further confirmation that my steps were being ordered at every turn. I was covered!

Victory does not always come by way of bright lights, shiny doors, or red carpets. There is always value in the quiet moments, sincere invitations, and the roads less traveled. You will need all your armor to break away from the light and trust that there are wins on the other side of the seemingly smaller moments.

THE BLOOM

Create your personal power chant! Find words that you can apply when you need to encourage yourself, when you are unable to see the light at the end of the tunnel, and when there is no evidence of a possible win!

Here are some of my courage-building phrases:

"There are no coincidences. This is bigger than you!"

"You are the *Yes!*"

"You were born of His greatness and nothing less!"

"Mediocrity is not of you!"

What will YOU say in those moments of uncertainty to boost your own confidence? This is your personal chant. Let's go!

CHAPTER 7

Big Breaks Are Not Convenient

Big Break: a breakthrough, especially the first big hit of a previously unknown performer in the entertainment industry

One late afternoon, I found myself running errands with my friend Lauren, a vegan chef who was in town to work with a few of her clients. One of our stops happened to be in the Hollywood Hills, but we arrived ahead of schedule and thought it best to wait in the car. She expressed a desire to perform and requested some of my vocal tips. So, while we waited, we began running vocal drills and warmups for about forty minutes. I cracked the car door open for more air circulation. It didn't give us much relief from the 80-degree temperature, but this was the only viable solution, since the windows had not been working properly on my 2001 sky blue BMW, and I couldn't keep the air conditioner running.

Once her client arrived home, I closed the car door, and we went inside for another 30 minutes, only to return to a vehicle that would not start! I knew my battery was a bit weak, but I didn't think it would totally fail me—or maybe I had failed it? I was unaware that during the time the door was cracked, the inside car light had silently killed my battery. Now, if this had been one of my "woe is me" moments, where I allowed the disappointing circumstances to emotionally overtake my body, I would have called a tow truck and ceased all activity for the remainder of the day. But to my surprise, I kept it moving.

To top it all off, my phone was of little use to me at exactly two percent battery life. It was just enough to call an Uber, charge the phone in the car, and rush to a date who was waiting for me at a restaurant in the Valley.

Within ten minutes of my arrival at the restaurant, I received a call from an unknown number. I didn't bother to answer because I was only taking calls from recognizable numbers and those which appeared to be urgent. The call was then followed by a text from Frank Gatson, a world-renowned creative director for artists such as Beyoncé, Kelly, Destiny's Child, Carl Thomas, Tyrese, Luke James, and several others. Most importantly, Frank was one of the executive producers of Kelly Rowland's new BET show, *Chasing Destiny*.

For context, I had been engaging both Stephen Hill (former President and Creative Executive of BET) and Frank Gatson for more than nine months regarding this particular show. It's safe to say I started my soft stalking tactics around June 2015, and by this point, it was January of 2016. I digress. Back to the story.

The message from Frank said to call him back asap. I turned to my date and said, "This is what needs to happen: I have to use your phone to take a photo of this number, call this guy Frank, and then call my mama for her AAA card number to fix my car. Are you good with that?"

He obliged, and I made all the calls. Frank asked, "Would you be available to come and meet Kelly Rowland in the next hour?"

I gave a resounding "Yes!", returned to the table, and said without hesitation to my date, "I've gotta go, but before we say goodbye, can you drive me back to my car and wait for AAA to come?"

He agreed, and now the evening began.

Upon my arrival, Frank introduced me to Kelly Rowland, the artist, songwriter, lyricist, dancer, actress, and executive producer, whose spirit is both generous and infectious. We had a quick yet meaningful conversation, and within 15 minutes, I was thrown into the studio with the contestants who were competing for the chance to form a new singing group, June's Diary.

Sidebar: No one knew about my last two hours, nor did it matter. They were expecting me to show up as what I professed to be, an artist development and performance expert.

I recalled my past workshops and extracted the most useful information while quickly assessing each performer. I began the work of challenging each girl to identify, embrace, and optimize her individual assets before attempting to contribute them to the collective.

Once this task was complete, Kelly acknowledged she wanted more of this type of work for herself. Frank responded by saying, "So, you *do* know what you're talking about!" This was exciting, especially since I have such a personal admiration for both Kelly and Frank.

Sometimes people can only see you through the lens they are most aware of. They may not be privy to your growth. Frank originally knew me as a back-ground singer, but I was presenting a new lens in the area of artist development. It wasn't his job to embrace this new career concept of mine, but it was my job to shift his perspective and just "be" what I was trying to make him see. This took a great deal of persistence and execution. I also had to deliver exceptional results!

The evening ended with Kelly saying, "Can you come back tomorrow?"

My immediate response was, "Absolutely."

Sometimes people can only see you through the lens they are most aware of. They may not be privy to your growth.

I arrived the following day thinking I would continue working behind the scenes as I had the previous evening, but I was mistaken. I walked in, and someone yelled, "Are we mic'ing KJ?"

Kelly confirmed with a strong "Yes."

I thought, *Who is Mike? Because I don't have on any TV makeup, eyelashes, or a lipstick that would translate well on camera.* But none of this vanity mattered. It was time to deliver. I swiftly ran to the bathroom and glanced into the mirror to make sure my hair was in place.

Before I knew it, the cameras were rolling. I stared at the three white stools in the center of the studio as the singers were seated in front, and through my own deductive reasoning, assumed those seats were assigned to Kelly, Frank, and me. However, I didn't want to be presumptuous and embarrassed if I was wrong. So, as we entered the room, I stayed behind to play it safe.

Kelly said, "KJ, this chair is for you."

Can you imagine how elated I was to hear those words? This experience reminded me of a sermon my Pastor, Dr. Lester W. Taylor Jr. of Community Baptist Church in Englewood, NJ had consistently preached: "Don't invite yourself to the table; wait to be summoned." Luke 14:10

It wasn't his job to embrace this new career concept, but it was my job to shift his perspective and just "be" what I was trying to make him see!

Oftentimes, there is a narrow space that exists between observing the moment and interjecting our expertise. I've learned that overtalking can be a detractor, which is more about the ego and our insecurities than anything else. Being able to discern those moments that are designated for listening is equally important. I was positioned as a collaborator to Kelly and Frank, which was a balance between listening and having something of value to contribute when called upon.

On this day, I filmed my very first docu-series, Kelly Rowland's *Chasing Destiny*. This seed had been planted and cultivated for almost ten months, and it had finally manifested. Consequently, my work on this show garnered a referral for my next project, E! Entertainment's *Revenge Body with Khloe Kardashian,* as an artist performance expert for her featured talent.

But let me remind you that an hour before all this awesomeness unfolded, I was immobile and almost unreachable. There are times we don't see the big break or opportunity because we expect it to be ushered in without difficulty. I believe this day was about preserving my joy despite the circumstances. It was my decision to remain optimistic amid the mishaps, which kept my possibilities flowing.

Every single second is directly connected. It is our response to those seconds that dictates our next opportunity, based purely on our perspectives. A negative attitude will adversely affect our next win. The times we identify as challenging and inconvenient are not intended to rob us of all the thrilling moments awaiting us.

THE BLOOM

Observe your most challenging experiences over the next three days and share your responses to them. There may be moments in which our responses do not completely serve us. Making a record of them ensures that we make better choices the next time. It keeps us aware. Don't judge yourself during this process; just honor your progress.

Day 1:

The Challenge:

_____

_____

_____

Your Response:

_____

_____

_____

Day 2:
The Challenge:

_____

_____

_____

Your Response:

_____

_____

_____

Day 3:
The Challenge:

_____

_____

_____

Your Response:

_____

_____

_____

CHAPTER 8

The Power of the Push-Through

Push-through: the ability to be excellent despite everything around you crumbling

I've been working with one of the most gifted, intelligent, and biggest breakthrough artists of this time, Lil Nas X. I firmly believe that we are divinely assigned to one another, to save one another.

One evening, I watched in awe as Quincy Jones presented Lil Nas with a Diamond Plaque for selling ten million copies of his song, "Old Town Road." I was like a doting aunt, as it has been an absolute privilege to witness and take part in his meteoric journey.

Immediately following the presentation of the plaque, we hopped in a sprinter van and headed to Palm Springs for LNX to shoot a Doritos commercial that would air during the Super Bowl, and this would be epic!

Day one of the commercial, I watched him push through these uncharted waters with grace and make the necessary adjustments in this expanded territory. Day two, spirits were high as we were singing and dancing in the trailer. I believed that this day would run smoothly.

By the afternoon, I received a call from my landlord, who hysterically told me that my home had been invaded, robbed, and ransacked. I bolted from the trailer and cried in disbelief. I quickly gathered myself as I noticed that LNX had been taken back to set, and I needed to be there. I raced to get to him while fighting back the tears with each stride.

When I landed on set, I encountered LNX's stylist, Hodo, who could see, even through my sunglasses, that I was absolutely shaken. I needed to hide this energy from LNX, as he is quite intuitive. I stood at the monitor to observe and encourage his performance, yelling, "Great job, Lil Nas!" as tears rolled down my face and Hodo held my hand in solidarity. In this moment, the paradox of experiencing my greatest high in the midst of my greatest violation was ever-present. They were occupying the same space.

Once I received the pictures of my home, my knees buckled, and in between takes of the commercial, I would sob on the side of the trailer to release the hurt so I could make room to be present for LNX. I needed him to be victorious in his performance, although I felt utterly defeated.

As the days passed, I realized that if it weren't for me delighting myself in my passion or being obedient to the call from Phylicia Fant, Co-head of Urban Music at Columbia Records, there was a strong possibility I might have been home during this invasion. My commitment to LNX was what pushed me to suggest two days in Palm Springs with him, as opposed to the initial mention of one.

It took me longer than I would have liked to recover from this ordeal. As I searched for the meaning of it all, I soon realized that I had been living but not thriving in my home. I was scared to move because I was consumed with a skewed narrative that I could not afford anything else, nor had I worked hard enough to deserve a home that resembled luxury. I made my decision to remain stagnant from a place of fear instead of trusting that I deserved God's full abundance. Although the other areas of my life were being elevated, I still couldn't release the notion that struggle was part of my narrative.

As painful as this felt, God needed to move me into position to receive every bit of his goodness. There are times we must push beyond the boundaries of our own feelings to honor the greater victory. When we fall short of fulfilling our assignments, we run the risk of thwarting God's plan for those who are meant to be blessed by our gifts.

So, whatever you desire to do in this life, please go hard and abide in your gift completely! I promise that your gift will *cover* you, it will *save* you, and it will *love* you back.

THE BLOOM

What skewed narratives are you holding onto?

_____

_____

_____

State the narrative that you desire; the one that serves you best.

_____

_____

_____

What is your *force*? What areas do you naturally come alive? What will you use to activate your push-through?

_____

_____

_____

IT'S GROWING SEASON

Your performance is merely an expression of your heart.

Nurture it, protect it, and THRIVE.

Complete the following sentence:

She _____; she *Rose.*

He_____; he *Rose.*

Love,

KJ Rose

SEEDS OF VICTORY

DON'T OUTSOURCE YOUR WIN!
(PRE-APPROVE YOURSELF)

DON'T WAIT TO ACCESS
THE ENERGY IN THE ROOM.
BRING YOUR OWN!

SHOW UP AND BE PRESENT!
NO ONE CAN SHOW UP FOR YOU.
NO ONE CAN SHOW UP LIKE YOU.

IDENTIFY AND ABIDE IN
YOUR FORCE!

NO MATTER WHAT, MAKE IT
COUNT. YOUR POINT OF VIEW.
YOUR DELIVERY. YOUR SPACE.
YOUR GIFT.

ENTER EVERY ROOM KNOWING
THAT YOU ARE THE SOLUTION.
YOU ARE THE YES!

DON'T DISMISS ANYONE. STAY
HUMBLE AND STAY OPEN!

GOD DOES NOT CALL THE QUALIFIED;
HE QUALIFIES THE CALLED.
BELIEVE THIS!

1 Corinthians 1:27-29

About the Author

Keanna "KJ Rose" Henson has established a distinguished career as a singer, writer, and artist. She is the founder of The Rose Effect, a global artist development and performance consultancy, and she has conducted workshops both nationally and globally (London, Ireland, and Australia). It is her creative density and infectious energy that companies like Adidas, OWN, Google, Univision, Pandora Media, L'Oreal, SXSW, Tri Destined Studios, AdColor, Omnicom Media, Nickelodeon, Disney, Pretty Girls Sweat Inc., Universal, Capitol, Warner Brothers, Columbia, and Rostrum Records find compelling as they deem her to be the "ultimate solution" for their talent.

Roseeffect.com
Instagram: kjroseeffect
To inquire about booking KJ Rose for a speaking engagement, please contact theroseeffectpr@gmail.com

NOTES

NOTES

NOTES

NOTES

NOTES

NOTES

NOTES

Made in the USA
Columbia, SC
02 April 2023

14661967R00062